digging in the dirt

A Kid's Guide to How Plants Grow

Patricia Ayers

The Rosen Publishing Group's
PowerKids Press™
New York

Published in 2000 by The Rosen Publishing Group, Inc.
29 East 21st Street, New York, NY 10010

First Edition

Book Design: Maria Melendez

Photo Credits: Cover and title page, pp. 1, 4, 5, 9, 10, 11 © Super Stock; pp. 1, 2, 4, 6, 7, 12, 13, 14, 17, 18, 21 © International Stock; p. 8 © FPG International.

Photo Illustrations: pp. 1, 12, 15, 16, 19, 20 © Michelle Davis

Ayers, Patricia.
       A Kid's guide to how plants grow / Patricia Ayers.
            p.   cm. — (Digging in the dirt)
       Summary: Briefly describes how different kinds of plants grow and reproduce, as well as their importance to life on Earth.
       ISBN 0-8239-5465-X (lib. bdg.)
       1. Indoor gardening Juvenile literature. 2. House plants Juvenile literature. [1. Plants.] I. Title. II. Series: Ayers, Patricia.
       Digging in the dirt.
       SB419.2.A94   1999
       635.9'65—dc21
                                                                                                              99-28910
                                                                                                                  CIP

Manufactured in the United States of America

Contents

Jungle Plants

Underwater Plants

Forest Plants

Cactus Plants

Power in Plants

Did you know that your life depends on plants? Plants put **oxygen** in the air for you to breathe. They also make food for animals and people to eat. Plants have been around for three billion years, which is longer than people have been around.

There are at least 350,000 different kinds of plants, from the tiny ones you can't see without a **microscope** to giant trees that make up forests and jungles. Plants grow under the sea, on mountain tops, and in the desert. Plants have even found ways to live where people can't live.

◀ *Plants have found a way to live in almost every place on earth.*

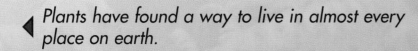

Making Themselves at Home

The first plants grew in water. As plants spread across the world, they found ways to live in all kinds of different places. To survive, they had to change a lot over the years. Cactus plants that lived in the desert got very little rain, so they grew fat bodies with extra room to store water. Their thick roots spread wide to collect what little water there was underground. Other plants grew into special shapes and sizes to help them survive in their different **climates**. Some plants even learned to grow without dirt! Tropical orchids, for example, can send roots out into the moist air to collect water and nutrients.

Cactus plants store water in their thick, fat bodies. ▶

Some Plants Bite Back

Have you heard of a plant that eats meat? Well, some do. Plants grow or change in order to live in a certain environment. Some plants, like the Venus's-flytrap, learned to eat meat because the soil where they lived didn't have enough of the **nutrients** they needed. These plants began to make a sweet smell to attract insects. Once an insect lands on the plant, it is trapped inside. The blossom of the Venus's-flytrap actually snaps shut around the insect. Others, like the pitcher plant, use sticky hairs or a pool of thick nectar to catch insects.

◀ *After the Venus's-flytrap catches an insect, it eats it.*

9

The Life Cycle

Plants do a lot to make our planet a healthy place to live. Cities use grass and trees to make the air easier to breathe. Plants have tiny holes in their leaves which take in the **carbon dioxide** that people breathe out. Then the plants release oxygen, which people need to breathe in. Plants also release water out into the air. This water enters the air, forms clouds, and returns to the earth as rain, watering the plants again. When plants die, they **decay**. As plants decay, they create nutrients that become part of the soil. This helps the plants to grow. This **cycle** is part of what keeps all living things alive.

Rain forests help keep the world a healthy place for people and animals. ▶

A World of Plants

Mr. Chavez's class decided to grow a little "world of plants" in the classroom. They would grow plants that came from different places, such as the desert cactus and the tropical fern. To start their project, they needed to find out what kind of climate and food each plant needed. The desert cactus plants would need a dry, hot spot, like near the heater or by the window, where a lot of sun could reach them. Tropical ferns need to feel like they're in the **rain forest**, with moist air and low light. The class decided to grow their tropical ferns in the bathroom, which they could keep warm and moist.

◄ *Tropical fern plants grow best in a warm and wet environment.*

13

Time to Plant

Mr. Chavez bought small desert cactus plants and tropical fern plants for the class to **transplant**. To start, the students filled pots with potting soil. They mixed in some **fertilizer**, which is rich in nutrients. Then they made a well in the center of the pot. The students transplanted the plants from their small plastic containers into the larger pots. They carefully set each plant into a pot, covered the roots with dirt, and watered the soil. Mr. Chavez told the class to water the plants right after transplanting to help them get used to being in a new place.

It's important to transplant plants into larger pots, so the roots have room to grow. ▶

Drink It Up!

Mr. Chavez told his class about the different water needs of their plants. The desert cactus plants needed water, but not too much water. The dirt had to dry out completely before being watered again. Students were told to water their desert cactus plants every 7 to 10 days. Cactus plants don't need to be watered all the time because they store water inside of their fat **stems**. The tropical ferns needed to be watered twice a week or whenever their dirt felt dry.

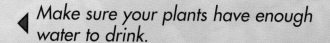

◀ *Make sure your plants have enough water to drink.*

Watching Plants Grow

The class watched their plants grow each day. They began to see changes. The stems of the desert cactus plants grew fatter and taller. The stems of the tropical ferns grew new stems and leaves. Next, buds appeared on the desert cactus plants. The buds opened up into beautiful little flowers. The class learned that certain cactus flowers open only at certain times of the day. There is even one type of cactus that blooms only at night. Tropical ferns do not grow buds or flowers. Instead they grow a lot of leaves. The students noticed that on the underside of the leaves were tiny black dots. These dots are called **spores**.

It's exciting to watch plants grow and blossom. ▷

Making More Plants

Most plants start as seeds. However, some plants grow from spores or **bulbs**. A spore is a special kind of cell that can grow into a new living thing. Ferns, mosses, and molds produce spores. A bulb is a thick plant-bud that is formed under the surface of the soil. When certain plants die for the season, their bulbs remain. The bulbs store food from the plant, and may **sprout** again the next year if the temperature is right. Sometimes plants grow a second or third bulb before they die. Tulips, lilies, and onions produce bulbs.

Not all plants start as seeds. Some plants come from spores and others come from bulbs.

What Plants Do For Us

Plants are the most important source of food for all animals. Many things humans eat, like fruits, vegetables, herbs, and grains, are all plants. Did you know that even some types of cactus can be eaten? Besides food, plants give us wood, oils, dyes to make colors, and oxygen to breathe. Look around you and you can see all the different things made from plants. This book you are reading is made from paper, which was once a living tree.

Glossary

bulbs (BULBZ) A thick plant-bud that is formed under the surface of the soil.

climates (KLY-mits) The weather conditions of a certain place; their temperature, humidity, winds, and rainfall.

carbon dioxide (KAR-bin dy-OX-side) A gas that plants take in from the air and use to make food.

cycle (SY-kel) A series of events that repeats itself in the same order again and again.

decay (dih-KAY) To rot.

fertilizer (FER-tuh-lyz-er) Material like manure, compost and chemicals, added to dirt to make it fertile, or healthy for plants to grow.

microscope (MY-croh-scope) An instrument with a lens used for making small things look larger.

nutrients (NEW-tree-ents) Something a living thing needs for energy, to grow, or to heal.

oxygen (OX-ih-jen) A gas that is part of the air. People and animals cannot live without it.

rain forest (RAYN FOR-est) A very wet area that has many kinds of thickly growing plants and trees.

spores (SPORZ) Special kinds of cells on the underside of certain plant leaves that the plant uses to reproduce.

sprout (SPROUT) To begin to grow.

stems (STEMZ) The main supporting part of a plant above the ground.

transplant (tranz-PLANT) To move from one place to another; replanting.

Index

Web Sites:

24

To learn more about growing plants, check out these Web sites:
    http://www.urbanext.uiuc.edu/gpe/index.html
    http://aggiie.horticulture.tamu.edukinder/funpage.html